House of Commons
Defence Committee

UK operations in Iraq and the Gulf

Fifteenth Report of Session 2007–08

Report, together with formal minutes

*Ordered by The House of Commons
to be printed 15 July 2008*

HC 982
Published on 22 July 2008
by authority of the House of Commons
London: The Stationery Office Limited

The Defence Committee

The Defence Committee is appointed by the House of Commons to examine the expenditure, administration, and policy of the Ministry of Defence and its associated public bodies.

Current membership

Rt Hon James Arbuthnot MP (*Conservative, North East Hampshire*) (Chairman)
Mr David S Borrow MP (*Labour, South Ribble*)
Mr David Crausby MP (*Labour, Bolton North East*)
Linda Gilroy MP (*Labour, Plymouth Sutton*)
Mr David Hamilton MP (*Labour, Midlothian*)
Mr Mike Hancock MP (*Liberal Democrat, Portsmouth South*)
Mr Dai Havard MP (*Labour, Merthyr Tydfil and Rhymney*)
Mr Adam Holloway MP (*Conservative, Gravesham*)
Mr Bernard Jenkin MP (*Conservative, North Essex*)
Mr Brian Jenkins MP (*Labour, Tamworth*)
Mr Kevan Jones MP (*Labour, Durham North*)
Robert Key MP (*Conservative, Salisbury*)
John Smith MP (*Labour, Vale of Glamorgan*)
Richard Younger-Ross MP (*Liberal Democrat, Teignbridge*)

The following Members were also Members of the Committee during the Parliament.

Mr Colin Breed MP (*Liberal Democrat, South East Cornwall*)
Derek Conway MP (*Conservative, Old Bexley and Sidcup*)
Mr Mark Lancaster MP (*Conservative, North East Milton Keynes*)
Willie Rennie MP (*Liberal Democrat, Dunfermline and West Fife*)
Mr Desmond Swayne MP (*Conservative, New Forest West*)

Powers

The Committee is one of the departmental select committees, the powers of which are set out in House of Commons Standing Orders, principally in SO No 152. These are available on the Internet via www.parliament.uk.

Publications

The Reports and evidence of the Committee are published by The Stationery Office by Order of the House. All publications of the Committee (including press notices) are on the Internet at: www.parliament.uk/defcom

Committee staff

The current staff of the Committee are Mike Hennessy (Clerk), Eliot Wilson (Second Clerk), Ian Rogers (Audit Adviser), Lis McCracken (Inquiry Manager), Richard Dawson (Committee Assistant), Christine McGrane (Secretary) and Stewart McIlvenna (Senior Office Clerk).

Contacts

All correspondence should be addressed to the Clerk of the Defence Committee, House of Commons, London SW1A 0AA. The telephone number for general enquiries is 020 7219 5745; the Committee's email address is defcom@parliament.uk. Media inquiries should be addressed to Alex Paterson on 020 7219 1589.

Contents

Summary

We visited Iraq and the Northern Arabian Gulf in June 2008, as part of our regular programme of scrutiny of the UK's major overseas operational deployments. It was a year since our last visit. In Basra, we found the security situation transformed. In 2007, there had been multiple and daily attacks on UK Forces in the Contingency Operating Base (COB), and we had been unable to venture outside the perimeter. We were told that UK Forces could only venture into the centre of Basra in strength and with considerable force protection. Those training and mentoring Iraqi Army units could not accompany those units on operations, which was hindering this work.

This year there had been an obvious and substantial improvement in security. UK Forces can now move freely in the city of Basra, and the Military Transition Teams which are assisting the Iraqi Army are now embedded with their units. We saw that this process is going well, and has already contributed enormously to the capacity of the Iraqi Security Forces. It seems clear to us that this is largely the result of the success of Operation Charge of the Knights, the Iraqi-led effort to break the control of the militias in Basra and restore law and order. The operation continues, but its effects are already profound and positive. We are concerned that the wider public does not see the very positive developments which we undoubtedly saw in Iraq. That is why we decided to publish this Report.

The training and development of the Iraqi Security Forces is now the most important task facing UK Forces in southern Iraq. We were enormously impressed with what we saw in Basra and at the Naval Training Team at Umm Qasr. It is however obvious that these are long-term projects. The MoD will have to consider how it adjusts its current military footprint in Iraq to accommodate a continuing and vital, if smaller, presence in both these places. The larger the military training commitment we can maintain, the greater will be UK influence in Iraq, and in the region as a whole, as Iraq recovers its position as a wealthy and powerful Middle East nation. The UK has an opportunity to maintain a substantial position of influence for the common good in southern Iraq, if we can commit the military capacity to do so.

We also visited Royal Navy units in the Arabian Gulf and saw the crucial task they have in defending Iraq's oil infrastructure there. Oil is the key to the future prosperity of Iraq, and helping the Iraqis ensure stability and security in the Gulf is a vital role for the Coalition. We pay tribute to the work that UK Service personnel are doing and recognise the often difficult, sometimes dangerous and always delicate nature of operations in that area.

Economic development will be the cornerstone of Iraq's prosperity and security. Iraq is not inherently a poor country, and the UK Government has the opportunity to help Iraq realise and reap the benefits of its potential wealth.

1 Introduction

1. The Defence Committee has carried out regular scrutiny of UK operations in Iraq (Operation TELIC) since forces were committed in 2003, and has undertaken frequent visits to the operational theatre since that date. During this Parliament we have visited Iraq in June 2006, July 2007 and June 2008. There have been four substantive Reports on the issue since 2004[1], and in addition we have scrutinised the Ministry of Defence (MoD) Main and Supplementary Estimates with a particular focus on the cost of operations both in Iraq and Afghanistan.

2. The purpose of this Report is to place on the public record a summary of our most recent visit to Iraq and the Northern Arabian Gulf and the conclusions reached by those of us who participated in the visit. In drawing up our observations, recommendations and conclusions, we have relied primarily on the first-hand experience of those Members, but also on the extensive information available in the public domain as well as our own previous Reports and the evidence submitted to them.

3. We want to place our observations on the record as quickly as possible, so as to provide a snapshot of the situation as we found it in Iraq and the Gulf. We will return to the issue later in the year and intend to take evidence from the Secretary of State for Defence and the Secretary of State for Foreign and Commonwealth Affairs among others. We are committed to continuing scrutiny of this significant deployment of UK Forces, and hope to return to Iraq in the summer of 2009.

---

1   Third Report of Session 2003-04, *Lessons of Iraq*, HC 57; Sixth Report of Session 2004-05, *Iraq: An Initial Assessment of Post-Conflict Operations*, HC 65; Thirteenth Report of Session 2005-06, *UK Operations in Iraq*, HC 1241; First Report of Session 2007-08, *UK land operations in Iraq 2007*, HC 110.

2 The security situation in southern Iraq

The situation in 2007

4. When we last visited Basra in July 2007, it was clear that the security situation was extremely fragile. We were unable to leave the Contingency Operating Base (COB) at Basra Air Station (unlike the previous year, when we had been able to visit UK Forces stationed in Basra Palace), and there were several rocket attacks each day and night on the COB during our stay. In 2007, there was a pervasive sense of pessimism among those whom we met, from the General Officer Commanding Multi-National Division (South East) (MND(SE)) downwards, and a belief that the UK had perhaps outstayed its welcome. The additional factor of increasing Iranian influence in southern Iraq had contributed to a significant escalation in violence during 2006–07.

5. Shortly after our visit, in September 2007, UK Forces handed over their base at the Provincial Joint Co-ordination Centre (PJCC) in Basra Palace to the Iraqi Army, leaving the COB, outside the centre of the city, as the only Coalition base. Reflecting this, by the time our Report on Iraq was published in the autumn of 2007, there had been a reduction in the number of attacks on UK and Coalition Forces in Basra. Nevertheless, the way forward remained unclear. We concluded:

> The fact that there has been no corresponding reduction in the number of attacks against the civilian population of the city is a matter of concern. Violence in Basra Province continues to undermine the development of civil society. The relative security of Basra is said to owe more to the dominance of militias and criminal gangs, who are said to have achieved a fragile balance in the city, than to the success of the Multi-National and Iraqi Security Forces in tackling the root causes of the violence.[2]

Meeting in Baghdad Ambassador Ryan Crocker and General David Petraeus, who briefed us on the first stages of the surge, we heard that positive results were beginning to appear, which threw the situation in Basra into sharp relief.

6. However, in 2007 we were told that the violence in southern Iraq was of a different nature from that in and around Baghdad. While the insurgency which Coalition Forces were facing in Baghdad was led by the nihilism of al-Qa'eda in Iraq (AQI)—a Sunni group—that in Basra was ultimately self-limiting, as it represented a competition for power and money between various Shi'a organisations (some of them Iranian-backed). Essentially, no party wanted to destroy that over which it sought to exert control.

Provincial Iraqi Control

7. On 16 December 2007, Basra became the last province in south-eastern Iraq to move to Provincial Iraqi Control (PIC), following Maysan, Dhi Qar and al-Muthanna.

[2] HC (2007–08) 110, para 41

8. We were told during our recent visit to Iraq that the situation immediately following Provincial Iraqi Control, while more stable than six months previously, had not shown significant improvement. With UK Forces moving to a supporting role, the burden had fallen on the Iraqi Security Forces. Militia strongholds in Basra had remained impregnable, with the ISF either unwilling or unable to enforce security in those areas of the city.

Operation Charge of the Knights

9. The turning point in the security situation in Basra seems to have come in March 2008. Lieutenant-General Mohan al-Furayji had been appointed head of the Basra Operational Command (BaOC) in 2007, thereby assuming control of all Iraqi Army forces in southern Iraq. One of his key decisions was the raising of the 14th Division of the Iraqi Army, based on 5 Brigade, 10th Division, as a unit specifically recruited from outside Basra (the soldiers of the locally-raised 10th Division had been subject to intimidation and infiltration by Basrawi militias). He also began preparations for a major offensive against the militias in Basra, telling one British journalist at the time of the transition to PIC that "The lawlessness in Basra is an insult to the Iraqi people and an insult to the Iraqi government. It simply cannot be tolerated".[3]

10. Moqtada al-Sadr and his followers in Jaish al-Mahdi (JAM) had renewed their ceasefire in February 2008, but the detention of so-called rogue members of JAM in the weeks following brought the stability of the ceasefire into question. In March, General Mohan warned his troops that decisive action against the militias would soon be necessary.[4] We were told during our visit that the operation, dubbed *Saulat al-Fursan* or "Charge of the Knights", had been planned for the summer months, in order to be concluded before the beginning of Ramadan in September and the provincial elections in Basra later in the autumn, but that the timeline was accelerated at the behest of the Iraqi Prime Minister, Nouri al-Maliki.

11. On 25 March 2008, Prime Minister al-Maliki arrived in Basra to oversee Operation Charge of the Knights personally. Full details of the tactical operations over the following days are not publicly known, nor is this the place to rehearse or speculate on them. However, according to reports in the press, JAM called for a ceasefire on March 30, with discussions being held in Iran.[5] By the following day, JAM units had ceased to appear openly on the streets and a semblance of normality had begun to return to Basra.

12. We visited the Basra Operational Command at the Shatt-al-Arab hotel during our recent visit, and met both Major-General Mohammed Juwad Huwaidi, who succeeded General Mohan as commander of Iraqi forces in May 2008, and the UK BaOC mentor, Colonel Richard Iron. We were told that Operation Charge of the Knights had resulted in a seismic shift in the balance of power between the ISF and the militias, and that a large part of its importance, apart from straightforward military success, lay in the fact that it had been conducted with Iraqi soldiers in the lead. There is no doubt that Coalition Forces provided essential support, both in terms of training, and in terms of heavy weapons and

---

3   "New Iraq receiving baptism of fire in Basra", *The Daily Telegraph*, 30 March 2008, www.telegraph.co.uk

4   "The final battle for Basra is near, says Iraqi general", *The Independent*, 20 March 2008, www.independent.co.uk

5   "Iraqi political effort targets al-Sadr", *USA Today*, 6 April 2008, www.usatoday.com

air cover, but the fact remained that it was Iraqi Security Forces which restored stability and security to the streets of Basra.

13. It is true that US Marines were also on the streets of Basra during this offensive, but this was not as an independent force. Prime Minister al-Maliki ordered in the Iraqi 1st Division as reinforcement. The US Military Transition Teams were embedded with the 1st Division, and providing additional operational planning, artillery support and tactical air support, significantly enhancing Iraqi military capability. This victory achieved a step change in Iraqi military self-confidence and transformed Prime Minister al-Maliki's political prestige. Moreover, the embedded US Marines were greeted by Basrawis, not as part of an occupying force, but as supporters of an increasingly capalble Iraqi Army.

14. Operations under the umbrella of Charge of the Knights continue. Some parts of Basra are still outside the full control of the ISF. Moreover, a new insurgency is likely to develop as militia groups adjust to the changing security situation. However, the ISF are creating increasingly sophisticated counter-insurgency tactics and apparatus, and economic growth in Basra is also likely to erode the appeal of the militias. The influence of Iran, however, remains a key factor. It is likely that Iran's strategic objectives in southern Iraq include keeping Coalition forces preoccupied with Iraq rather than with broader regional issues. We were told that these objectives have not been altered by the success of Operation Charge of the Knights, and the fact that the border between southern Iraq and Iran remains porous allows militias and weaponry to flow easily from one country to another.

15. However, it will be increasingly difficult for JAM and the Sadrist movement to re-establish its former dominance. The provincial elections in southern Iraq, due late this year, offer Moqtada al-Sadr an opportunity to establish a political power base in and around Basra, but he and his movement cannot participate in the elections while JAM remains an avowed militia movement. Sadr therefore must find a way to distance himself from JAM or change the identity of JAM if he is to engage in the political process.

16. **We are reassured that Operation Charge of the Knights has been broadly successful, and has substantially weakened the power of the militias in Basra. While some areas of the city are not yet fully under the control of the ISF, a high degree of security has been restored and the preconditions are in place for political progress and economic recovery. There is no doubt that more remains to be done. The UK Government must ensure that it continues to provide support to the ISF to ensure that the progress which has been made is not lost and that Basra does not slip back into instability.**

Divisional Internment Facility

17. We visited the UK-run Divisional Internment Facility (DIF) in the COB. This has been a continuing matter of interest to us. We were told that the facility operates in accordance with international and domestic law. Those being held are a mixture of internees and detainees. The DIF is scrutinised by the International Committee of the Red Cross and by the Army's Provost Marshal, and complaints are dealt with by the Special Investigation Branch.

18. The power to intern derives from United Nations Security Council Resolution 1637. If there is no resolution after the current one expires in December 2008, the UK will stop the

internment process. However, the improving security situation in Basra is likely to make the process much less necessary. The future of the DIF is uncertain, but it may be that an arrangement can be reached bilaterally with the Iraqi government or under the aegis of the Long-Term Security Arrangement being negotiated by the United States.

3 Development of the Iraqi Security Forces

19. It is clear to us that one of the most important tasks now facing UK and Coalition Forces in southern Iraq is the development of the capability of the Iraqi Security Forces. The Prime Minister told the House of Commons in October last year that "in the Spring of next year [2008] [...] we plan to move to a second stage of overwatch where [...] the main focus would be on training and mentoring".[6] This is undertaken in three main areas: the training and development of the Iraqi Army, of the Iraqi Police Service, and of the Iraqi Navy.

Military Transition Teams

20. UK Forces undertake the training and development of the Iraqi Army in southern Iraq through the use of Military Transition Teams (MiTTs). These teams, usually of 20–30 UK Service personnel, work alongside the Iraqi units. In July 2007, we visited the MiTT which was working with the 10th Iraqi Division and was based inside the COB. We heard that the 10th Division was already largely recruited, partly accommodated, largely equipped, partially sustained and largely trained, and that equipment shortfalls were due to difficulties in extracting resources from the Iraqi Ministry of Defence (IMOD). The Commanding Officer of the MiTT stressed to us then that its work was done within the COB and that members of the team did not go out on operations with the Iraqi army units, because it was not possible to provide force protection for them.

21. We encountered a transformed situation in June of this year. The Commanding Officer of the MiTT Group told us that there were currently 11 MiTTs, comprising around 1,000 personnel drawn from the Royal Scots Dragoon Guards, 4th Battalion, The Royal Regiment of Scotland, 2nd Battalion, The Royal Anglian Regiment, and 9th/12th Royal Lancers. The MiTTs are a combination of a core of 20–30 trainers, headed by a major or a lieutenant-colonel, and a small force protection unit of around 60 which allow the teams to deploy operationally alongside the Iraqi units which they are training. Crucially, the UK MiTTs are now based with their 'parent' Iraqi units outside the COB.

22. The approach of the MiTTs is two-fold: to help develop the Iraqi Army's capabilities, and to help defeat the militias. This second strand has only been possible because of the improved security situation, which has allowed the MiTTs to operate outside the COB without requiring unmanageable levels of force protection. An important aspect of the first strand is enhancing the Iraqi Army's own training capability, referred to as "training the trainer". The MiTTs have found that Iraqi personnel tend to mimic the behaviour they see in the UK personnel training them. It is also important to try to move towards the Iraqis taking a lead in training and mentoring to avoid creating a culture of dependency.

23. We were also briefed by the Commander Force Support. He explained that UK Forces were helping to foster the development of a capable ISF logistics system through the use of Logistics Training and Advisory Teams within MiTTs. During Operation Charge of the Knights, the UK had provided considerable logistical support to the ISF, including water,

food, petrol, diesel and JP8 jet fuel. The new Commander of Multi-National Corps-Iraq, Lieutenant-General Lloyd J. Austin III, had made it clear that he did not want logistics problems to inhibit ISF operations. Progress had so far been slow, and there were particular problems in terms of long-term maintenance of equipment by the Iraqis. However, these problems were not unique to the ISF and were being addressed. The Logistics Training and Advisory Teams were beginning to have an effect, though second-line ISF logistics units were yet to be generated.

24. The UK MiTTs are doing an excellent job in enhancing the capacity and self-sufficiency of the Iraqi Army. Their work is vital to the future of the Iraqi Security Forces and therefore to stability in southern Iraq. The contrast with what we saw last year is stark and profound, and the MoD must continue to support the MiTTs in what will inevitably be a medium-to long-term project. The larger the military training commitment we can maintain, the greater will be UK influence in Iraq, and in the region as a whole, as Iraq recovers its position as a wealthy and powerful Middle East nation. The UK has an opportunity to maintain a substantial position of influence for the common good in southern Iraq, if we can commit the military capacity to do so.

The Iraqi Police Service

25. When we visited Iraq in July 2007, we were told that, while the Iraqi Army was progressing reasonably well, substantial shortcomings remained in the Iraqi Police Service (IPS). There were high levels of corruption and militia infiltration in the IPS, and the fact that UK and Coalition Forces were all-but confined to the COB made any real progress very difficult. The Iraqi government had demonstrated its determination to improve the situation by appointing Major-General Abdul Jalil Khalaf as Chief of Police in Basra, but he had not at the time of our visit been able to make much headway. He told a British journalist later that year that he was exposed to almost daily assassination attempts.[7]

26. Operation Charge of the Knights put Basra in the spotlight both nationally and internationally. We heard anecdotal claims that the performance of the IPS had been patchy at best, and that perhaps as little as a third of the police in Basra had stood its ground and defended the police stations against militia attacks. We were also told that, in the wake of Charge of the Knights, significant numbers of IPS personnel had been dismissed for collaboration and corruption, including a large number of senior officers.

27. A new Chief of Police, Major-General Adel Dahaam, was appointed in April 2008. We were told that, although he comes from a military background, he wears a police rather than army uniform, unlike his predecessor, and we were briefed on his plans to reform the IPS apparatus in Basra.

28. The UK Police Mission in Iraq, based in Baghdad and Basra, has switched its focus from a tactical level to a strategic, national project to help build capacity in the IPS and the Iraqi Minister of the Interior. Its priorities are:

- Strategic development, including the devolving of power where appropriate;

---

7 "Basra: The Legacy", *BBC News Online*, 17 December 2007, www.bbc.co.uk

- Tackling corruption and working with the Iraqi Department of Internal Affairs to improve its capabilities;

- Leadership training at Shaibah Police College, using a Danish model of training which has been employed successfully in Kosovo and other places, and

- The development of forensic capabilities, including the opening of a national crime laboratory in Basra.

29. An important feature of the UK effort, because of its small size, is cooperation with the US mission and the creation of a common plan across Multi-National Force-Iraq. This is delivered through the Civilian Police Assistance Training Team, based in Baghdad. However, one limitation on the UK Police Mission is the resources available to it. The UK lacks a gendarmerie-style police force and so cannot deliver the full range of training and support which the IPS needs. The US, by contrast, will employ some Military Police units to provide training.

30. **The UK Police Mission is a small component of Coalition efforts in developing the IPS. We were impressed by the work it is doing and by the systematic and organised nature of its plans, and hope it can continue to provide valuable support to the IPS. We also hope that the Police Mission can extend its reach and enhance its training capacity as the security situation in Basra becomes more stable.**

Joint Security Stations

31. An important part of the security strategy for the ISF in southern Iraq is the Joint Security Station concept. These 'hub-and-spoke' establishments will be based on existing IPS command-and-control units, and will incorporate elements from the IPS, the Iraqi Army, MiTTs and Police Transition Teams. They are intended to allow the IPS to use the Iraqi Army as an 'enabler' and to enhance the counter-insurgency capabilities of the ISF. Importantly, they build on existing capabilities and provide a post-Coalition framework for the development of the ISF.

Naval Training Team

32. The UK-led Naval Training Team (NaTT) based within the Iraqi Navy compound at the southern Iraqi port of Umm Qasr is made up of around 75 personnel from all three UK Services, the US Navy and the US Marine Corps. Its mission is to mentor, monitor and train the Iraqi Maritime Forces, both Navy and Marines. Umm Qasr has vital strategic and economic importance to Iraq. It is the country's only deep-water port, and the Iraqi Navy's only significant gateway to the Northern Arabian Gulf.

33. When we visited the NaTT in July 2007, we were briefed on ambitious plans to expand the Iraqi Navy to more than double its size in terms of personnel by 2010 and to undertake a major procurement project. When we returned in June 2008, we were told that the plans, while challenging, were still broadly on course. The Iraqi Navy's current capability was described as adequate with the vessels and equipment already in Iraqi hands. There are also plans to redevelop the base at Umm Qasr. This will be a vital part of enhancing the Iraqi Navy's capabilities, as many of the buildings are currently in poor condition.

34. The two main challenges facing the Iraqi Maritime Forces are the undefined nature of Iraq's territorial waters, especially in relation to Iran, and the protection of the two off-shore oil platforms, the al-Basra Oil Terminal (ABOT) and the Khawr al-Amaya Oil Terminal (KAAOT). These are vital to the economic success of Iraq, as they account for around 90% of the country's revenue.

35. The issue of Iraq's territorial waters is complex and contentious. Under United Nations Security Council Resolution 1723, the UK is mandated to patrol the Shatt-al-Arab waterway and the mouth of the Northern Arabian Gulf. This brings them into close contact with Iranian naval units, Iran disputing the border of its territorial waters with Iraq. There have been two major clashes with Iranian units, in June 2004 and March 2007, which have led to the seizure of UK personnel by Iranian forces.[8]

36. We visited the smaller KAAOT platform during our recent visit to the Gulf and were briefed on the strategic and economic importance of the oil platforms as well as the security measures in place to protect them. While the principal burden of providing defence falls on UK personnel, the Iraqi Maritime Forces are assuming an increasing share of the responsibility. We saw how Iraqi Marines work alongside UK and US Forces in defending the oil platforms. We consider this further in Chapter 4, below.

37. **The UK-led Naval Training Team is performing a vital role in training and mentoring the Iraqi Navy, and we pay tribute to the excellent work which UK Forces are doing at Umm Qasr. It is clear to us that the mission of the NaTT is a long-term one, and, while we understand that the UK Government may not wish to make public pronouncements on future dispositions in Iraq, we encourage the MoD to consider how a UK presence can be maintained in Umm Qasr beyond any drawdown of forces in Basra.**

8   For the latter, see Defence Committee, Fourth Report of Session 2007-08, *The Iran hostages incident: the lessons learned*, HC 181 and Foreign Affairs Committee, Sixth Report of Session 2006-07, *Foreign Policy Aspects of the Detention of Naval Personnel by the Islamic Republic of Iran*, HC 880

4 Naval operations

38. Our previous Reports on UK operations in Iraq have tended to focus on the land component. This has simply been a consequence of the relative weight of numbers, but we noted in our most recent Report on the subject that:

> The fact that this report does not comment on the progress of maritime operations in Iraqi waters is not a reflection of the relative importance we attach to these operations. We acknowledge the important contribution which all three Services are making to the security of the region.[9]

39. However, our focus was already being drawn increasingly to the maritime component of UK operations with the seizure by Iranian naval units of Royal Navy and Royal Marine personnel in March 2007. In the wake of the hostage crisis, and following the report on the matter by Lieutenant-General Sir Rob Fulton, we conducted a private inquiry into the issue, and in December 2007 published a Report, as well as writing in confidential terms to the Secretary of State for Defence.[10] Consequently, when we came to plan our visit to Iraq and the Gulf in 2008, we were eager to include a greater concentration on UK maritime activities in our programme.

40. We visited the Coalition Maritime Component Command in Bahrain and met both Vice-Admiral Kevin Cosgriff, US Naval Central Commander (USNAVCENT) and Commander of the US Fifth Fleet (COMFIFTHFLT), and Commodore Keith Winstanley RN, UK Maritime Component Commander (UKMCC) and Deputy Coalition Force Maritime Component Commander (DCFMCC). They briefed us on the full scope of Coalition naval operations in the Arabian Gulf.

41. The Arabian Gulf is covered by US Central Command (CENTCOM), the area of responsibility (AOR) of which encompasses 27 countries.[11] The supply and distribution of oil is a critical priority for CENTCOM, given the relative vulnerability of the two Iraqi oil platforms and the fact that the Arabian Gulf has certain obvious 'choke points'. We were told by Vice-Admiral Cosgriff that NAVCENT's primary focus is Iran, and that US relations with Iran were difficult, but that there had been some progress made.

42. The mission of the UKMCC is to provide "tasking and logistical support to RN Units within an operational area of over 2.5 million square miles, 24 hours a day, 365 days a year".[12] At the time of our visit, the UK provided the lead for two Coalition Task Forces, CTF 158 (Northern Arabian Gulf) under the command of Commodore Duncan Potts RN and CTF 152 (Central and Southern Arabian Gulf) under the command of Commodore Peter Hudson RN.

---

9   HC (2007–08) 110, para 12

10   HC (2007–08) 181

11   Afghanistan, Bahrain, Djibouti, Egypt, Eritrea, Ethiopia, Iran, Iraq, Jordan, Kazakhstan, Kenya, Kuwait, Kyrgyzstan, Lebanon, Oman, Pakistan, Qatar, Saudi Arabia, Seychelles, Somalia, Sudan, Syria, Tajikistan, Turkmenistan, United Arab Emirates, Uzbekistan, and Yemen; however, all the countries in Africa with the exception of Egypt will fall within the remit of the new US African Command (AFRICOM) when it becomes active later in 2008.

43. CTF 158's area of responsibility includes the ABOT and KAAOT oil platforms as well as the border between the territorial waters of Iraq and Iran, and its efforts are focused in the north-western corner of its AOR. Its work complements that of the NaTT in pursuing the goal of a self-sufficient Iraqi Navy. It is also engaged in demining operations, as well as attempting to resolve the territorial disputes between Iraq and Iran. We were told that the Iraqi Navy is increasingly capable and takes the lead in perimeter defence at Umm Qasr, as well as contributing Iraqi Marines to the defence of the oil platforms.

44. **The work of UK and Coalition maritime forces in the Northern Arabian Gulf is crucial to the security and economic prosperity of Iraq, as well as to wider regional stability. We pay tribute to the work that UK Service personnel are doing and recognise the often difficult, sometimes dangerous and always delicate nature of operations in the area.**

5 Economic development in southern Iraq

45. It is clear to us that the establishment of security in southern Iraq and the development of the Iraqi Security Forces is only one link in the chain of rebuilding Iraq. The creation of economic prosperity is an essential accompaniment to security, and will in turn contribute to it. The area has enormous economic potential due to its massive natural resources, but these must be efficiently and effectively harnessed.

46. The economy in Basra is difficult to assess at the current time. There are perhaps more than 10,000 small businesses, many operating at the fringes of legality. Equally, it is difficult to estimate accurately the level of unemployment, but one source told us that it is as high as 90%. This is a massive and pressing challenge. It is clear, however, that Basra has enormous economic potential because of its strategic location in terms of shipping and its role in the oil industry.

47. During our recent visit, we met Mr Munadhil Abid Khanjar, the co-Chairman of the Basra Development Committee. He told us that the overall security situation in Basra, which had improved immeasurably as a result of Operation Charge of the Knights, was acceptable, and that the improvement was already having an economic impact. Major companies were exploring the possibility of investing in the city, and unemployment was falling, though it remained a significant problem. We also met a number of local Basrawi politicians. They reinforced the message that economic development and the alleviation of unemployment were now the overriding priorities, given the improvement of the security situation.

48. We were also briefed on the reconstruction and development efforts of the Coalition. Funding for these projects derives from a number of sources, and in several areas in southern Iraq it is UK Forces delivering effects funded by US money. Two major funding streams are the Commander's Emergency Response Program (CERP), which is paid for by the US, and the Iraqi counterpart, I-CERP, which uses revenue from Iraqi sources. Many of the projects which are supported from these sources use local labour and work through traditional tribal hierarchies.

49. The UK operates a Provincial Reconstruction Team (PRT) in Basra, the only UK-led PRT in Iraq. Unlike the US-led teams, which are embedded with a brigade combat team, the Basra PRT is separate from the military. It is headed by the Foreign and Commonwealth Office but also draws staff from the Department for International Development. The primary focus of the Basra PRT is on working with the provincial government to access and prioritise existing Iraqi funds and implement good governance. Many of the staff have served comparatively long tours, up to three years, and so often know their Iraqi counterparts well.

50. The different streams of funding and development generally separate by mission. The military-led teams are concentrating on short-term tactical projects. This is intended to buy time in which longer-term projects can be carried out both by the PRT and by local government structures. Assistance from the US Agency for International Development (USAID) fall within the purview of the PRT.

51. Another important factor in the economic revival of Basra will be the handing over to Iraqi control of Basra International Airport, which we were told is scheduled for later in 2008. When we visited Basra in July 2007, we were told that the commercialisation of the airport, which had begun in early 2005, was proceeding slowly but steadily, with between 150 and 200 civilian air movements each month, both passenger and freight. This important work is continuing. We were shown round the airport during our recent visit, and the signs of progress were evident. **It is important that the 'civilianisation' of Basra International Airport continues, and the UK Government must take account of this in any plans to draw down UK Forces and to reorientate the COB.**

52. **Economic prosperity and increasing security and stability are inextricably linked. The proper harnessing of oil revenues will provide the Iraqi government with an invaluable source of income, which will in itself contribute to the development of the ISF. At the same time, growing prosperity and the reduction of unemployment in Basra will have a serious impact on the popularity of the militias. Unemployment and poverty are among their greatest recruiting sergeants. Iraq is not inherently a poor country, and the UK Government has the opportunity to help Iraq realise and reap the benefits of its potential wealth.**

Conclusions and recommendations

1. We are reassured that Operation Charge of the Knights has been broadly successful, and has substantially weakened the power of the militias in Basra. While some areas of the city are not yet fully under the control of the ISF, a high degree of security has been restored and the preconditions are in place for political progress and economic recovery. There is no doubt that more remains to be done. The UK Government must ensure that it continues to provide support to the ISF to ensure that the progress which has been made is not lost and that Basra does not slip back into instability. (Paragraph 16)

2. The UK MiTTs are doing an excellent job in enhancing the capacity and self-sufficiency of the Iraqi Army. Their work is vital to the future of the Iraqi Security Forces and therefore to stability in southern Iraq. The contrast with what we saw last year is stark and profound, and the MoD must continue to support the MiTTs in what will inevitably be a medium-to long-term project. The larger the military training commitment we can maintain, the greater will be UK influence in Iraq, and in the region as a whole, as Iraq recovers its position as a wealthy and powerful Middle East nation. The UK has an opportunity to maintain a substantial position of influence for the common good in southern Iraq, if we can commit the military capacity to do so. (Paragraph 24)

3. The UK Police Mission is a small component of Coalition efforts in developing the IPS. We were impressed by the work it is doing and by the systematic and organised nature of its plans, and hope it can continue to provide valuable support to the IPS. We also hope that the Police Mission can extend its reach and enhance its training capacity as the security situation in Basra becomes more stable. (Paragraph 30)

4. The UK-led Naval Training Team is performing a vital role in training and mentoring the Iraqi Navy, and we pay tribute to the excellent work which UK Forces are doing at Umm Qasr. It is clear to us that the mission of the NaTT is a long-term one, and, while we understand that the UK Government may not wish to make public pronouncements on future dispositions in Iraq, we encourage the MoD to consider how a UK presence can be maintained in Umm Qasr beyond any drawdown of forces in Basra. (Paragraph 37)

5. The work of UK and Coalition maritime forces in the Northern Arabian Gulf is crucial to the security and economic prosperity of Iraq, as well as to wider regional stability. We pay tribute to the work that UK Service personnel are doing and recognise the often difficult, sometimes dangerous and always delicate nature of operations in the area. (Paragraph 44)

6. It is important that the 'civilianisation' of Basra International Airport continues, and the UK Government must take account of this in any plans to draw down UK Forces and to reorientate the COB. (Paragraph 51)

7. Economic prosperity and increasing security and stability are inextricably linked. The proper harnessing of oil revenues will provide the Iraqi government with an

invaluable source of income, which will in itself contribute to the development of the ISF. At the same time, growing prosperity and the reduction of unemployment in Basra will have a serious impact on the popularity of the militias. Unemployment and poverty are among their greatest recruiting sergeants. Iraq is not inherently a poor country, and the UK Government has the opportunity to help Iraq realise and reap the benefits of its potential wealth. (Paragraph 52)

Annex: List of abbreviations

ABOT	al-Basra Oil Terminal
AOR	Area of Responsibility
AQI	al-Qa'eda in Iraq
BaOC	Basra Operational Command
CENTCOM	United States Central Command
CERP	Commander's Emergency Response Program
COB	Contingency Operating Base
COMFIFTHFLT	Commander of the United States Fifth Fleet
CTF	Coalition Task Force
DCFMCC	Deputy Coalition Force Maritime Component Commander
IMOD	Iraqi Ministry of Defence
IPS	Iraqi Police Service
ISF	Iraqi Security Forces
JAM	Jaish al-Mahdi
KAAOT	Khawr al-Amaya Oil Terminal
MiTT	Military Transition Team
MND(SE)	Multi-National Division (South East)
MoD	Ministry of Defence
NaTT	Naval Training Team
PIC	Provincial Iraqi Control
PJCC	Provincial Joint Co-ordination Centre
PRT	Provincial Reconstruction Team
UKMCC	United Kingdom Maritime Component Commander
USAID	United States Agency for International Development
USNAVCENT	United States Naval Central Commander

Formal minutes

Tuesday 15 July 2008

[Afternoon Sitting]

Members present:

Mr James Arbuthnot, in the Chair

Mr David Crausby MP	Mr Bernard Jenkin MP
Mr Mike Hancock MP	Robert Key MP
Mr Dai Havard MP	

Draft Report (*UK operations in Iraq and the Gulf*), proposed by the Chairman, brought up and read.

Ordered, That the Report be read a second time, paragraph by paragraph.

Paragraphs 1 to 52 read and agreed to.

Annex (List of abbreviations) and Summary agreed to.

Resolved, That the Report be the Fifteenth Report of the Committee to the House.

Ordered, That the Chairman make the Report to the House.

Ordered, That embargoed copies of the Report be made available, in accordance with the provisions of Standing Order No. 134.

[Adjourned till Tuesday 7 October at 10.00 am

List of Reports from the Committee during the current Parliament

The reference number of the Government's response to each Report is printed in brackets after the HC printing number.

Session 2005–06

First Report	Armed Forces Bill	HC 747 (*HC 1021*)
Second Report	Future Carrier and Joint Combat Aircraft Programmes	HC 554 (*HC 926*)
Third Report	Delivering Front Line Capability to the RAF	HC 557 (*HC 1000*)
Fourth Report	Costs of peace-keeping in Iraq and Afghanistan: Spring Supplementary Estimate 2005–06	HC 980 (*HC 1136*)
Fifth Report	The UK deployment to Afghanistan	HC 558 (*HC 1211*)
Sixth Report	Ministry of Defence Annual Report and Accounts 2004–05	HC 822 (*HC 1293*)
Seventh Report	The Defence Industrial Strategy	HC 824 (*HC 1488*)
Eighth Report	The Future of the UK's Strategic Nuclear Deterrent: the Strategic Context	HC 986 (*HC 1558*)
Ninth Report	Ministry of Defence Main Estimates 2006–07	HC 1366 (*HC 1601*)
Tenth Report	The work of the Met Office	HC 823 (*HC 1602*)
Eleventh Report	Educating Service Children	HC 1054 (*HC 58*)
Twelfth Report	Strategic Export Controls: Annual Report for 2004, Quarterly Reports for 2005, Licensing Policy and Parliamentary Scrutiny	HC 873 (*Cm 6954*)
Thirteenth Report	UK Operations in Iraq	HC 1241 (*HC 1603*)
Fourteenth Report	Armed Forces Bill: proposal for a Service Complaints Commissioner	HC 1711 (*HC 180*)

Session 2006–07

First Report	Defence Procurement 2006	HC 56 (*HC 318*)
Second Report	Ministry of Defence Annual Report and Accounts 2005–06	HC 57 (*HC 376*)
Third Report	Costs of operations in Iraq and Afghanistan: Winter Supplementary Estimate 2006–07	HC 129 (*HC 317*)
Fourth Report	The Future of the UK's Strategic Nuclear Deterrent: the Manufacturing and Skills Base	HC 59 (*HC 304*)
Fifth Report	The work of the Committee in 2005 and 2006	HC 233 (*HC 344*)
Sixth Report	The Defence Industrial Strategy: update	HC 177 (*HC 481*)
Seventh Report	The Army's requirement for armoured vehicles: the FRES programme	HC 159 (*HC 511*)
Eighth Report	The work of the Defence Science and Technology Laboratory and the funding of defence research	HC 84 (*HC 512*)
Ninth Report	The Future of the UK's Strategic Nuclear Deterrent: the White Paper	HC 225–I and –II (*HC 551*)
Tenth Report	Cost of military operations: Spring Supplementary Estimate 2006–07	HC 379 (*HC 558*)

Printed in the United Kingdom by The Stationery Office Limited
7/2008   405694   19585